I0222509

But, the *Holy Ghost*

A Journal for the
Paragraphs You Deleted

Righteous Write Hand Publishing

Dedication

*To anyone who often feels alone and has no one to reason with,
God is a God of justice. He is the best vindicator, and the truest
friend. While, He's working out your situation, work out your
salvation. Make every effort to live peaceably with all men,
including yourself! "Encourage yourself in the Lord" is not a
glamorous place to live, but I'm glad you're living. Keep living!
You will find peace while you process, and revelation will come
from heaven. Bless you!*

Introduction

Throughout your lifetime, you'll experience intense emotions such as hurt, rejection, unfair judgments, false accusations, etc. It can come from total strangers, your closest friend, or anyone in between. In these times, prayer should be our first line of defense. In some instances, prayer provides immediate relief.

In other instances, resolve manifests at an appointed time in our future. Between the time we said our prayers and the resolve, our human emotions may still be on a level of intense. It is during this time that there is a real temptation to sin, whether in word or deed. While our emotions are very real and very valid, there is still a standard of righteousness ordained by God that requires us to be angry and sin not (Ephesians 4:26). This begs the question: how can we reconcile our very real and raw emotions with the standard of God?

First, we must become aware of ways to acknowledge our emotions and care for our souls righteously. We know that journaling is one way we can healthily value and process our emotions. Additionally, journaling is another form or bringing our raw emotions to the Father, and receiving revelation about a situation. Often times David took a pause from people, God alone with God, and brought his raw emotions to the Lord. The Lord would respond to David and deposit revelation into him about who he is, and the outcome of the very situations he was praying about; this would encourage David, and has often encouraged many of us.

Second, we must build this righteous strategy into our life routine, whether it be daily weekly, biweekly, monthly, etc. Set a regular time/date to deal with all your emotional baggage. Life can get real. Additionally, we must be conscious that our journal is still valuable outside of our routine. Always use your journal to address frustrating situations that catch you by surprise.

In both of these instances: (1) whether a part of your daily routine, or (2) if a situation tempts you to send a vexed text, update a Facebook status, Tweet a read, Snapchat a subliminal, or Instagram an insult, this journal is a great resource to help you process. You get to post your status to heaven's social media, and receive updates in the form of revelation. You can shout right there!

This journal belongs to

_____

Date_____

What's on Your Mind?

What's on Your Mind?

What's on Your Mind?

What's on Your Mind?

What's on Your Mind?

What's on Your Mind?

What's on Your Mind?

What's on Your Mind?

What's on Your Mind?

What's on Your Mind?

What's on Your Mind?

What's on Your Mind?

What's on Your Mind?

What's on Your Mind?

What's on Your Mind?

What's on Your Mind?

What's on Your Mind?

What's on Your Mind?

What's on Your Mind?

What's on Your Mind?

What's on Your Mind?

What's on Your Mind?

What's on Your Mind?

What's on Your Mind?

What's on Your Mind?

What's on Your Mind?

What's on Your Mind?

What's on Your Mind?

What's on Your Mind?

What's on Your Mind?

What's on Your Mind?

What's on Your Mind?

What's on Your Mind?

What's on Your Mind?

What's on Your Mind?

What's on Your Mind?

What's on Your Mind?

What's on Your Mind?

What's on Your Mind?

What's on Your Mind?

What's on Your Mind?

What's on Your Mind?

What's on Your Mind?

What's on Your Mind?

What's on Your Mind?

What's on Your Mind?

What's on Your Mind?

What's on Your Mind?

What's on Your Mind?

What's on Your Mind?

What's on Your Mind?

What's on Your Mind?

What's on Your Mind?

What's on Your Mind?

What's on Your Mind?

What's on Your Mind?

What's on Your Mind?

What's on Your Mind?

What's on Your Mind?

What's on Your Mind?

What's on Your Mind?

What's on Your Mind?

What's on Your Mind?

What's on Your Mind?

What's on Your Mind?

What's on Your Mind?

What's on Your Mind?

_____

_____

_____

_____

_____

_____

_____

_____

_____

_____

_____

_____

_____

_____

_____

_____

_____

What's on Your Mind?

What's on Your Mind?

What's on Your Mind?

What's on Your Mind?

What's on Your Mind?

What's on Your Mind?

What's on Your Mind?

What's on Your Mind?

What's on Your Mind?

What's on Your Mind?

What's on Your Mind?

What's on Your Mind?

What's on Your Mind?